DISCOVER
Weather

Contributing Writer
David A. R. Kristovich, Ph.D.

Consultant
Robert W. Grumbine, Ph.D.

D1391130

Publications International, Ltd.

Louis Weber, C.E.O.
Publications International, Ltd.
7373 North Cicero Avenue
Lincolnwood, IL 60646

Photo Credits

Front cover: **Comstock** (center); **National Center For Atmospheric Research**
(bottom right).

Back cover: **Tom & Michele Grimm/International Stock Photography** (bottom); **D.
Marklin/FPG International** (top).

FPG International: 29 (center), 37 (top); Floyd Dean: 18 (bottom); D. Dietrich: 15 (top);
Kenneth Garrett: 32 (top); Gebhardt: 12 (top & center); Dave Gleiter: 4 (top); Steve
Gottlieb: Back endsheet (top left); Peter Gridley: 40 (top left); Jeffry W. Myers: 16 (top);
E. Nagele: 38 (center); Stan Osolinski: 43 (center); Terry Qing: Front endsheet (top left),
7 (bottom); Steve Raye: 21 (top); Jerry Sieve: 29 (top); R. Hamilton Smith: 10 (bottom
left); Latin Stock: 9 (bottom); M. Stoklos: 28 (bottom); Jeffrey Sylvester: 28 (top), 30
(center); J. Taposchaner: 43 (bottom); The Telegraph Colour Library: Contents (top), 6
(top), 8 (top); L. West: 38 (top), 42 (bottom); Jack Zehrt: 13; **International Stock
Photography:** James Davis: 21 (right center); Warren Faidley: Front endsheet (top right);
Bob Firth: Front endsheet (center), 19 (center); Michele & Tom Grimm: 16 (bottom);
Richard Hackett: 17; Stephen S. Myers: 21 (left center); Wilson North: 18 (center); Horst
Oesterwinter: 21 (bottom), back endsheet (top right); Richard Pharaoh: 40 (top right);
Spencer Photo: Back endsheet (center); Tom Till: 9 (top left); **NASA/Weatherstock:** 1,
10 (bottom right), 36 (top), 40 (right center); **National Center For Atmospheric
Research:** 6 (center & bottom), 8 (center & bottom right), 14 (bottom), 19 (top), 25 (top,
left center, right center & bottom right), 29 (bottom), 33 (bottom left & bottom right), 37
(center); **Glenn M. Oliver/Eagle River Media Productions:** Contents (bottom left &
bottom right), 14 (center), 16 (center), 26 (top & center), 30 (bottom), 41 (bottom), back
endsheet (bottom left); **Glenn M. Oliver/Rainbow:** 5; **Weatherstock:** 15 (bottom left),
24 (bottom), 34 (top), 35 (center), 42 (top right); W. Balzer: 35 (bottom); M. H. Black:
Front endsheet, Contents (left center); Keith Brewster: 4 (center), 30 (top), 32 (bottom
right), 34 (center); J. Christopher: 24 (top & center); Warren Faidley: Front endsheet;
(bottom left), Contents (right center), 4 (bottom), 7 (top), 8 (bottom left), 10 (top), 14
(top), 18 (top), 26 (bottom), 27 (top), 31, 32 (bottom left), 33 (top), 38 (bottom), 39, 41
(center), 43 (top); M. Laca: 15 (bottom right); Mike Magnuson: 11, back endsheet
(bottom right); Gary McCracken: 37 (bottom), David R. Olsen: 36 (bottom), 42 (top left
& center); Lawrence M. Sawyer: 34 (bottom); Joe Towers: 27 (center); John W. Warden:
9 (top right), 19 (bottom); Kent Wood: 7 (center), 25 (bottom left), 27 (bottom left &
bottom right).

Illustrations: Lorie Robare; Steve Fuller

David A. R. Kristovich is a visiting lecturer in the Physics Department at University of
Illinois at Chicago teaching meteorology. He was previously a research associate in the
Cloud Physics Laboratory at University of Chicago working in boundary-layer
meteorology and cloud microphysics.

Robert W. Grumbine is a physical scientist at the National Meteorological Center. He
formerly researched climate-ocean interaction at Pennsylvania State University and has
written numerous articles on climate.

CONTENTS

OUR WEATHER • 4

Weather is an important part of our everyday lives. While everyone has an interest in the weather, not many people really know how it works.

CHANGES IN THE ATMOSPHERE • 10

Weather is what the air around us is like. The forces that change the air are the forces that create our weather.

WATER IN THE ATMOSPHERE • 16

Water is probably the most active part of our atmosphere. Without it, there would be no life on Earth.

CLOUDS IN THE SKY • 22

Clouds bring us rain and snow. They are good clues about what weather is on the way.

THUNDERSTORMS, TORNADOES, AND HURRICANES • 30

The fury and power of a violent storm can be quite frightening. Weather is sometimes a dangerous thing.

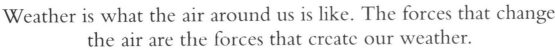

STRANGE AND BEAUTIFUL SIGHTS • 38

Sunsets, rainbows, and brilliant blue skies are just a few of the artworks that weather can create.

GLOSSARY • 44

OUR WEATHER

affects everyone. For some, the weather might mean that they have to plant a certain kind of crop or that they must hurry to bring in the hay. For others, the weather can make their normal 15-minute drive to work take an hour.

The weather can delay a baseball game or ruin a picnic, and it can make a day at the beach perfect.

The weather can bring peace and contentment with a shimmering sunset or a brilliant rainbow. It can also bring fear and grief with a violent hurricane or a deadly tornado.

People want to know if it's going to rain today or if it will be sunny over the weekend. They want to know what it will be like next year and when their children grow up.

4

The density of the air near the ground is one of the things that makes the weather change so much. Conditions high in the atmosphere also affect the weather.

Climbers sometimes feel out of breath on top of very high mountains because there is less oxygen there.

This computer-generated model (above) shows areas of high pressure. The atmosphere above a high pressure system is much denser than the atmosphere above a low pressure system. This drawing (right) shows typical wind patterns across the globe. Winds move mainly because of differences in air pressure and temperature.

Weather is what the air around us is like at a certain time. This might mean the weather at two o'clock today or the weather predicted for tomorrow morning. When we think of the weather, we usually think of things like hot and cold, cloudy and sunny, or rain and snow. The air around us has many other qualities, too. The pressure of the air and the amount of gases and dust particles it holds can tell a lot about what the weather will be like. What happens in the air high above the ground also affects conditions near the ground.

Air surrounds Earth like a thick blanket. We call this blanket the *atmosphere.* We all live most of our lives at the bottom of this blanket of air, and the weight of all the air rests on us. The air near Earth's surface gets pressed down by the air above it. This is a lot like what happens to a sponge when you hold it in your hand and squeeze it. The sponge gets *denser* or more solid when you squeeze it and less dense when you let go of it. You always have the same amount of sponge, but it's packed tightly and fills less space when you squeeze it.

In the same way, the air near the surface is squeezed by the weight of all the air above it, so it is quite dense. The air becomes less dense as you move farther and farther away from the ground. When you get very high in the atmosphere, there is very little air left.

Earth's atmosphere contains many different kinds of gases and dust particles. Most of the air within 50 miles of the ground is a gas called nitrogen. Less than a quarter of the air is oxygen. The air also has argon, carbon dioxide, and many other gases. The atmosphere also contains many kinds of dust particles that are important to weather patterns.

Weather is what the air is like at a certain time, and it changes from day to day. But how can we describe changes in the weather that occur over a whole year, over a decade, or over your lifetime? *Climate* is the term that describes the weather during a long period of time.

Studying climate is similar to looking at the grade you receive in a class over a whole year. You might have trouble with one homework assignment or one test, and that will affect your grade. If you do well on your other work, though, you'll still get the same kind of grade you usually do. In the same way, your area might have one really hot summer or one very rainy spring. That doesn't mean that your climate has changed. Conditions in the years before and after the unusual seasons will be normal, and your climate over all that time will be the same.

The air has some qualities that are not obvious, but they are very important to understanding weather.

Tiny particles such as salt enter the air when water evaporates from rivers, lakes, and oceans. Pollution from factories and cars also adds particles to the air. Water droplets form around these particles. The droplets then group together to make clouds. Without these tiny particles, our skies would have almost no clouds.

7

OUR WEATHER

Satellites are important tools for studying weather systems.

We use many different measurements to describe the weather. Each measurement requires a piece of special equipment. *Temperature* tells us how hot or cold it is. We measure temperature with *thermometers*. *Humidity* is the amount of moisture in the air, and we measure it with *hygrometers*. *Anemometers* measure the speed and direction of wind near the ground. *Atmospheric pressure*—the weight of the air in a certain area—is usually measured by *barometers*.

We take measurements like these at thousands of locations around the world every hour at ground level. Weather balloons carry equipment that measures temperature, humidity, and wind at different heights in the atmosphere.

All this information goes to major weather centers across the world for processing and storing. The centers use complex computer programs to help predict the weather. These programs use equations to describe rules about the way air

In the United States, the National Weather Service collects information from weather stations (left) all around the country.

The satellite photos you see on your local news programs probably come from the National Meteorological Center in Camp Springs, Maryland.

moves. With such programs, meteorologists can make very accurate forecasts of weather for the next few days for almost any area of the country or the world.

Some scientists have studied what Earth's climate was like in the past. The atmosphere came from inside Earth billions of years ago. Violent volcanoes, cracks, and fissures in the planet's crust shot gases from deep underground. Gravity kept the gases from escaping, and they eventually surrounded Earth.

Scientists have also studied how the atmosphere has changed since it first appeared. They've looked at weather as it is today, at rocks and fossils, at changes in the continents and oceans, and at air bubbles trapped by ice thousands of years ago.

Predicting what the climate will be like in the future is a very difficult but very important task. Generally, scientists believe that global temperatures will rise by the turn of the century. Pollution, deforestation, and other things that people have done will be the main cause. No one really knows when or how much the temperatures will change. Climate changes will probably mean that we will have to make changes in where and how we live.

Scientists have learned that Earth had no permanent ice at the Poles for most of its history. Conditions everywhere were too warm for ice and snow to stay on the ground year round like they do today.

When the atmosphere first formed, it was quite different from the atmosphere we see today.

Trees help keep the balance of gases in the atmosphere, and they affect the natural water cycle. By studying weather, we learn how our actions today could affect our world in the future.

9

CHANGES IN THE ATMOSPHERE create our weather. Air swirls, water changes from a gas to a liquid to a solid, and energy keeps it all moving around. Weather is an active, lively thing.

It may seem odd that the weather in one area usually changes slowly. When it turns cold in Minnesota,  it stays that way for a day or two. When it gets hot in Florida, it can stay that way for a few weeks. It usually doesn't turn cold and then hot and then cold again within a few minutes or even a few hours. When a snow storm is on the way, clouds might fill the sky for as long as two days, and the snow might last just as long.

Weather is an active thing but it's also a big thing, and that is why it seems slow to change.

10

The seasons are a result of Earth's tilt and its path around the sun.

Every day we see the sun rise and set, and it sends its heat to Earth. Of course, the sun doesn't really travel across our sky. Actually, it's Earth that moves. Our planet spins on an imaginary line called the axis that runs through the North and South Poles. This spinning makes it seem to us like the sun is moving overhead each day.

Earth's axis does not point straight up and down. Instead it is tilted a bit. The axis always tilts in the same direction, but Earth also travels around the sun. This means that sometimes the North Pole is tilted toward the sun and the South Pole tilts away from the sun. Other times it's just the opposite: The South Pole is tilted toward the sun and the North Pole is tilted away from it.

All this has a big effect on Earth's weather. When a part of the planet leans toward the sun, it gets more sunlight than it does at other times of the year. The ground absorbs the heat from this and passes it on to the air.

If that were the whole story, then places near the Equator would always be warmer than places away from the Equator. Also, the temperature would warm steadily as summer came and then cool steadily as winter came. Weather isn't that sim-

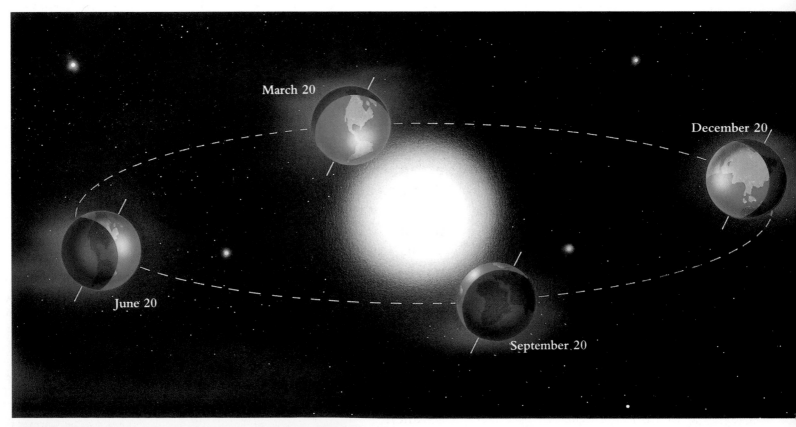

From about March 20 to September 20, the Northern Hemisphere leans toward the sun and has spring and summer. In the Southern Hemisphere, the seasons are reversed. The Equator gets direct sunlight year round, so it's always warm there.

A cold front forms when a cold air mass pushes into a warm air mass and forces the warm air up. Both cold fronts and warm fronts often create stormy weather.

ple though, mainly for two reasons. Not all of Earth's surface gets warmed the same amount by the sun, and air doesn't stay in one place.

Several things can affect how much the sun warms a patch of ground. The number of clouds in the sky, how high up the ground is, the number of plants or the amount of cement on the ground, and other things can make a difference. The biggest difference is that some areas are land and others are water. Land areas warm up much faster than water areas.

When air stays over a cold place for a long time, it cools and forms a bubble or dome of cold air. We call this a *cold air mass*. When a warm dome of air forms over a warm area, we call it a *warm air mass*.

Earth's spin, differences in the air's temperature, and other things make air masses move, and that also affects weather. If a cold air mass moves over your area, the temperature will become cooler. If a warm air mass moves over where you live, the temperature will go up.

When a cold air mass and a warm air mass move close to each other, a wall called a front forms between them. When the cold air mass is advancing, we call the wall a *cold front*. When the warm air mass is advancing, we call the wall a *warm front*.

As you move away from the Equator and toward the poles, areas spend less of the year getting direct sunlight and average temperatures are lower. Temperatures also change as you go from the continents to the oceans. This satellite image shows that land areas tend to be warmer than water areas.

13

CHANGES IN THE ATMOSPHERE

Barometers can gauge the air pressure very precisely. They provide one of the most useful measurements for making weather forecasts.

Some people say that you can catch more fish when it is raining. If you like to go fishing, you might like low pressure systems better than high pressure systems.

Clouds like these often form along fronts because the air is rising. Large, bumpy clouds usually form when the air rises quickly. Wide, layered sheets of clouds cover the sky when the air rises slowly.

Air pressure has a lot to do with the way that fronts and air masses act. Put simply, air pressure is the amount of push you feel on your body from the weight of the air around you. If you dive into the water, your body feels like it's being squeezed a little. The squeezing is because of the water's pressure. Air presses against us the same way, but we are used to feeling the air's pressure so we don't notice it.

Warm and cold air masses usually have a lot of pressure, so we call them *high pressure systems*. In high pressure systems, the air is slowly moving downward from high in the atmosphere. Clouds usually form in air that is moving upward, so high pressure systems almost always have clear skies.

Fronts have less air pressure than the air masses that they separate. Once in a while, an area of much lower pressure, called a *low pressure system,* forms along a front. Low pressure systems are the centers of storms that can be hundreds of miles across. The air in low pressure systems is moving upward into the atmosphere, so there are usually clouds and rain or snow near them.

Measuring the air pressure can tell a lot about what kind of weather to expect. In general, clear weather usually occurs in high pressure systems and stormy weather usually occurs in low pressure systems.

Wind direction also affects what kind of weather is coming. Wind is simply what we call moving air. The most important thing that causes the air to start moving is pressure differences. Air tries to make the pressure equal everywhere by moving from high pressure systems toward low pressure systems.

Wind power is one way that people can harness weather's great energy.

The wind tries to move in a straight line from the high pressure system to the low pressure system. Instead, it curves away because Earth rotates underneath it. Imagine that you have a record turning on a record player and you have to draw a line from the center of the record to the edge. If you moved your hand straight from the edge to the center, the line would curve around the record. In the same way, Earth's spin causes the wind to curve.

Most of the time, Earth's spin turns the wind so much that the air simply circles around the high and low pressure systems.

If you looked at a high pressure system in the Northern Hemisphere from above, you'd see that the wind has a clockwise rotation. Around a low pressure system, you'd see the wind turning in the opposite direction that a clock's hands move. This wind has counterclockwise rotation. In the Southern Hemisphere, the wind directions are just the opposite. Wind in high pressure systems spins counterclockwise. Wind in low pressure systems has clockwise rotation.

The bigger the difference in pressure between the systems and the closer the systems are, the stronger the wind will be.

15

WATER IN THE ATMOSPHERE

and on the ground comes in different forms. It can be a gas, a liquid, or a solid. We can run a steam engine, slide across the top of a lake on winter days,  and wash in a shower all using the same thing—water.

Because water changes form so much, it is a very active part of the atmosphere and is an important part of our weather. Water is the source of snow, ice, rain, and dew. Water also causes clouds to form and makes the air humid.

 Temperature has a big effect on the water in our atmosphere. Temperature is actually what causes water to change from a solid to a liquid to a gas. Working together, water and temperature bring us cool spring showers, eerie fogs, muggy summer days, and sparkling snowy landscapes.

16

The easiest way to understand what water molecules do in each state is to think about what you can do with water in each state. You can pass your hand easily through misty vapor, let water run through your fingers, or hold an ice cube.

The atmosphere has water in it, but water doesn't act like the other parts of the air at all. It's always changing and always moving. Water comes in three forms or *states*. When it is a gas, we call it *vapor*. When it is a liquid, we call it *liquid water* or just *water*. When it is a solid, we call it *ice*.

Like all things, water is made of tiny particles called *molecules*. The state that water is in depends on what these molecules are doing at the time.

 The molecules in a piece of ice are very organized and closely attached to each other. They don't move around much, and it's easy for you to handle them.

 In a liquid state, the molecules in water are not as well organized and only some of them are stuck to each other. The molecules are moving around more, and it's harder for you to handle them. Liquid water changes its shape easily and flows from one place to another. It will take the shape of whatever container it is in.

In vapor, the water molecules are the least organized and almost none of them are stuck together. The molecules move around a lot, and it is hard for you to handle them. You need a well-sealed container to capture water vapor.

The state that water is in depends mainly on temperature. When the temperature is below 32°F, water turns to ice. Water above 212°F turns to vapor. Between these temperatures, water takes the form of a liquid. Other things can affect the state that water is in, too. For example, small amounts of water will turn to vapor even when its temperature is below 212°F. As a general rule, though, these temperatures are the changing points.

When the temperature of water goes up, the molecules have more energy, so they move around more and are less likely to stick together. As the temperature goes down, the molecules have less energy, they move around less, and they are more likely to stick together.

At any given time, nearly all Earth's water is in the liquid state. About 97 percent of it is in rivers, lakes, swamps, and oceans. Two percent of the water is ice frozen in snow, glaciers, and the ice caps at the North and South Poles. Only one percent is vapor, but this tiny amount is very important to the weather.

Water is always changing from one state to another. Ice from glaciers falls in the sea and turns into liquid water as it floats to warmer areas. Water from oceans and lakes evaporates in the heat of the sun and becomes vapor in the atmosphere. Vapor in the atmosphere cools into water and forms clouds, fog, rain, and snow.

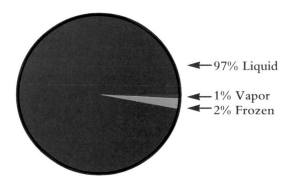

← 97% Liquid

← 1% Vapor
← 2% Frozen

Temperature changes the state of water because it changes the way the molecules act. Temperature is a measure of heat, and heat is energy.

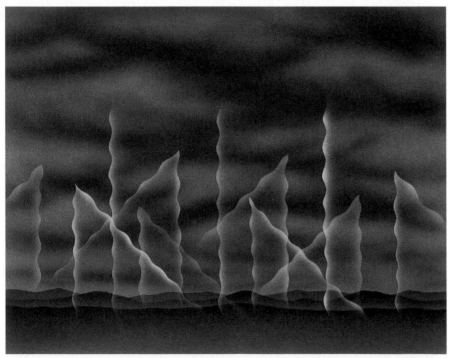

On clear nights (top), heat escapes from the ground easily. Clouds (above) can keep heat from escaping. On cloudy nights, it usually takes longer for the ground and the air above it to cool. Desert areas often get very cold at night because conditions there let heat escape easily. Deserts get a lot of heat during the day, but they are also very dry. No water means no clouds, and no clouds means all that heat escapes into space at night and leaves the area very cool.

Water vapor is always in the air, but the exact amount is always changing. The temperature of the air determines how much water vapor can be in the air. When it's warm, more vapor can stay in the air. When it's cold, there is less vapor. Think of the air as a bucket that changes size as it changes temperature, and think of water vapor as water in the bucket. When it's warm, the air is like a large bucket that can hold a lot of water. When it's cold, the air is like a small bucket that can hold less water.

Relative humidity is the amount of vapor that *can be* in the air compared to the amount of vapor that *is* in the air. If the relative humidity is 50 percent, the air has half as much vapor as it can hold. If it's 100 percent, the air can't hold any more vapor. When the humidity is more than 100 percent, some vapor condenses into liquid water. Two things make this happen; either more vapor enters the air, or the air cools down so it can hold less vapor.

Air near the ground gets colder if the ground beneath it gets colder. The most common way for the ground to cool is by radiating heat into space. During the day, the ground gathers heat from the sun. At night when the sun is gone, the heat escapes into space. First the ground loses its heat to space by radiation. Then the cold ground cools the air above it.

The other way for air to cool is by passing over ground that is already cold. This happens a lot in winter when winds in a warm air mass blow over an area that has snow on the ground. It also happens near large bodies of water because the water is usually colder than the nearby ground.

If the air near the ground cools enough, some of the water vapor in the air will condense into liquid water. Tiny droplets of water form on almost anything on the ground. This is called *dew*, and it is the reason

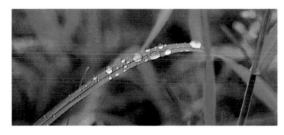

grass is often wet in the morning even though it hasn't rained.

If the temperature is below 32°F, dew will freeze into tiny ice crystals called *frost*. A frost in the fall is often the first sign that winter is coming.

Sometimes, winds in an area mix up the air so that even the air hundreds of feet up is cooled by the ground. Vapor condenses around tiny particles in the air and forms a thick, swirling mist called *fog*. Sometimes a fog can blanket an area for many days.

All of the threads in a spider's web can be seen when there is dew on it, as if nature decorated it with shining silvery beads.

Frost on a house's windows can add a pretty border to the view. Frost can also cover a car's windshield or cause damage to plants and farm crops.

Thick, heavy fogs often form over lakes and bays when the water is much cooler than the nearby land.

Clouds in the Sky

form every day. Sometimes we don't even notice them, and other times they capture our attention and start us daydreaming. It can seem as though nature made each one carefully by hand, using a white paintbrush to add decorations to the blue sky. They sometimes look like dragons, dogs, cats, trees, or fluffy pillows floating high overhead. Just look up in the sky when there are bulging clouds or light, wispy ones and see what kinds of things you can see.

Clouds form in the same way as fog and dew. Water vapor in the air condenses into liquid water. Conditions in the atmosphere when the clouds form have a lot to do with the shape and size of the clouds. This means clouds are an excellent clue for figuring out what conditions high in the sky are like. Sometimes you can tell what kind of weather to expect by studying the clouds.

22

Temperatures are typically colder at higher elevations. When warm, moist air is forced up over a mountain range, water condenses and forms clouds. Mountains sometimes have clouds and rain or snow, even when it is sunny just a few miles away.

Clouds form in much the same way that dew and fog form. Air cools down and can't hold as much water vapor. The water vapor then condenses into tiny droplets of liquid water.

You can get some idea of how clouds form by watching them. Many clouds, such as the thunderstorm cloud, look like they are made of bubbles, each pushing to get out of the cloud.

Most clouds form in bubbles that are rising in the air. When cloud bubbles are able to rise easily, like a beach ball rising to the top of a swimming pool, the air is *unstable*. The air is *stable* when bubbles of air can't rise easily, more like rocks that would sit on the bottom of a swimming pool.

Air moves up through the atmosphere for different reasons. It will rise if it runs into a large obstacle on the ground such as a mountain. When the air hits the mountain, it has to go up.

The atmosphere has its own obstacles that can make the air rise. The atmosphere has large areas of warm or cold air called air masses. The borders between these air masses are called fronts. As the air masses move, air is forced up and over the fronts. This is probably how most clouds form.

If you took one step for every droplet in a thunderstorm cloud, you'd be able to walk to the sun and back.

24

When bubbles of air rise into the atmosphere, the air gets colder and colder. Because colder air can't hold as much water vapor, some of the vapor condenses on dust particles. Billions of these dust particles enter the air when winds blow dirt and sand, when ash and smoke from fires rise in the air, and when cars and factories release pollutants. The vapor builds up on the dust particles and makes tiny cloud droplets.

The cloud droplets are so small that you can't see them. You can see the clouds because each one has so many cloud droplets. If you could grab a bucketful of cloud, you'd be holding as many as a quarter of a million cloud droplets.

If the air gets cold enough as it rises, the cloud droplets may begin to freeze and form ice crystals. These ice crystals have many different shapes and sizes and they help rain to form in the cloud. You can tell the

difference between a cloud of water droplets and a cloud of ice crystals by looking at them. The water droplet clouds usually look like they have hard, clear edges. The ice crystal clouds usually have soft, fuzzy edges.

These computer-generated images show a typical thunderstorm cloud as it forms. In the real world, it would take about 60 minutes for the cloud to develop.

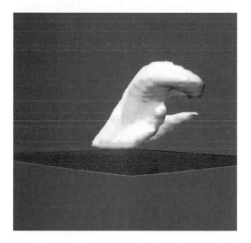

When you see stratus clouds getting thicker and covering more and more of the sky, you might be in for a long period of rain or snow.

You can sometimes tell what kind of weather is coming by looking at the clouds.

When cumulus clouds are getting taller and their bottoms are getting darker, you might be in for a short period of heavy rain, lightning, or even strong winds and hail.

Even though all clouds form in basically the same way, there are some differences between them. Conditions in the atmosphere can affect the way the air moves, and that can affect the way that clouds form. We can put most clouds into two groups. *Cumulus* clouds are bumpy and look like a pile of cotton balls. *Stratus* clouds are usually flat, they don't have many bumps, and they may cover a large portion of the sky.

These two kinds of clouds look very different because the air in them is moving in different ways. The air bubbles in cumulus clouds are rising very quickly, like bubbles in a pot of boiling water. The air moves up quickly and the clouds take on the shapes of the rising bubbles. This makes cumulus clouds look bumpy and bulgy. These types of clouds might form within a couple of hours during warm summer afternoons, when the air is unstable.

The air in stratus clouds is also rising into the atmosphere, but it is rising much more slowly. Because of this, the clouds tend to spread out horizontally, and they look flat. These kinds of clouds form when the air is more stable, and they may stay over your area for days. Stratus clouds form as the air rises over a warm front. They also form in low pressure systems, especially in fall and winter.

There are also different types of cumulus clouds and different types of stratus clouds. The names of different clouds in each group tell you a little more about the cloud. In the cumulus group, small clouds that are not very far from the ground and do not grow very deep into the atmosphere are just plain *cumulus* clouds. *Altocumulus* clouds are a little higher in the atmosphere, and they look a lot smaller to people on the ground. *Cirrocumulus* clouds are very high up in the atmosphere. In the same way, low clouds in the stratus group are called *stratus* clouds. When they are a little higher up, they are *altostratus*, and when they are very high, they are *cirrostratus*. If rain or snow is falling from cumulus clouds, they are

Cirrus clouds are a third group made mostly of ice crystals. These scattered, wispy clouds form at very high altitudes.

called *cumulonimbus*. Raining clouds in the stratus group are called *nimbostratus* clouds.

Of course, clouds aren't always this simple. You might see a cloud that looks flat and spread out like a stratus cloud, but it also has some places in it that bulge up into the sky like a cumulus cloud. A *stratocumulus* cloud is one cloud like this.

Some clouds don't really fit into either of the two cloud groups.

Large stratus clouds that you might see in winter low pressure systems often have parts where the air suddenly rises very quickly. A few cumulus clouds might form here and there within a large area of stratus clouds.

27

After about a million cloud droplets join together, a raindrop might be big enough to fall all the way to the ground.

The droplets in a cloud are very, very small. For water to fall to the ground, the clouds have to make drops that are big and heavy.

Clouds can make drops large enough to reach the ground in a few different ways. One way that raindrops form is when the cloud droplets run into each other and stick together. This process is called *coalescence*. Raindrops can also grow if water vapor continues to condense on them. As the vapor turns to water, it condenses on droplets in the cloud and the droplets can eventually become big enough to fall.

Clouds are actually made of tiny water droplets. These droplets are the water that helps make rain and snow.

As raindrops fall through the air, the air pushes upward on the bottoms of the drops. This forces the water in the drops to spread out so that the drops look a lot like hamburger buns. Raindrops don't always stay in that shape, though. Very often, they actually change back and forth between shapes. One instant they look like a hamburger bun with the flat side down, and the next they look like a football that's standing on its end. Raindrops seem to sparkle as they pass by a street light because the light bounces off them in a different direction each time they change shape.

The dark streaks coming from the bottoms of these clouds are actually rain.

28

Snow grows almost in the same ways that raindrops grow. Sometimes cloud droplets will freeze into tiny ice crystals if the air is very cold. These tiny snowflakes grow very fast when there are also cloud droplets near-by. When this happens, the cloud droplets evaporate and become water vapor and this vapor condenses onto the snowflakes, making them larger.

As the snowflakes grow, they also begin to fall downward through the cloud. Just like raindrops, they might run into more vapor as they go down and grow larger. Snowflakes can also run into cloud droplets as they fall. The droplets freeze and stick to the snowflake, and the snowflake gets bigger. This process is called *riming*.

Snowflakes come in two basic shapes. The shape of the snowflake depends mainly on the temperature of the air when the snowflake grew.

Columnar flakes are long and thin. They look a lot like sewing needles. Flat flakes are *planar* flakes. Planar snow-flakes usually have six arms, although once in a while they have 12 arms. If you see one that doesn't have six or 12 arms, some of them probably broke off as the flake was falling to the ground. Planar snowflakes actually come in a couple of different shapes.

Large snowstorms often form in the same way that large rainstorms do.

Flat plates (left) look like dinner plates, except that they're flat and have six sides. *Dendrites* (below) may be the most common type of flakes, and they're probably the most beautiful. Each of the six arms is shaped like a tiny Christmas tree.

Some people say that no two snowflakes are ever exactly the same. This may be true, but all snowflakes have some things in common about their shapes.

29

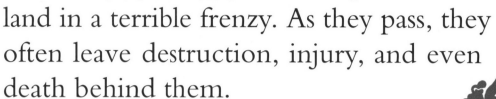

THUNDERSTORMS, TORNADOES, AND HURRICANES can be frightening.

Most of us will never see anything more powerful than one of these storms. They can sweep across the

land in a terrible frenzy. As they pass, they often leave destruction, injury, and even death behind them.

These storms may seem very scary and cruel, but they are a natural part of our weather. They are caused by the same processes that control our climate and change the seasons.

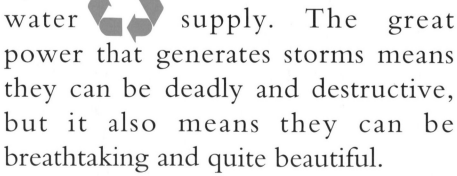

They are also a necessary part of our world. Storms are important to life on Earth because they recycle 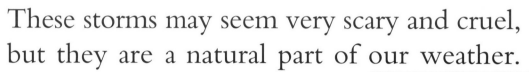 our fresh water supply. The great power that generates storms means they can be deadly and destructive, but it also means they can be breathtaking and quite beautiful.

30

Thunderstorms occur at one time or another in almost every part of the world.

Even though we are all used to them, thunderstorms can be very severe. Most of the time they just pass by without causing any real problems. Once in a while, though, a thunderstorm can damage trees, buildings, and almost anything that happens to be in its path.

Thunderstorms form when air rises very quickly into the atmosphere. Air rises when it is heated by the ground, when a front is approaching, or when the air is forced to move over a mountain or a hill. Clouds form in the rising air. These clouds can climb very high into the atmosphere. Clouds that are high enough to cause thunderstorms are called cumulonimbus clouds. The bottoms of cumulonimbus clouds are often very close to the ground, but their tops can stretch up several miles.

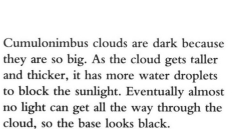

Cumulonimbus clouds are dark because they are so big. As the cloud gets taller and thicker, it has more water droplets to block the sunlight. Eventually almost no light can get all the way through the cloud, so the base looks black.

Rain, snow, and hail often form in cumulonimbus clouds, even though they may not always reach the ground. They can evaporate as they fall. Hail probably forms in most thunderstorms, but it usually doesn't reach the ground. In some parts of the world, the air is so dry that people see thunderstorms with no rain at all.

Severe thunderstorms can be dangerous for several different reasons. Lightning is a surge of electricity moving within a cloud, from one cloud to another, or from a cloud to another object. It can strike with no warning, and it can be very dangerous if you are close by. Lightning can strike anywhere, but will usually hit tall objects, such as trees or towers.

Another danger in thunderstorms comes from the rain. Heavy rains can cause flooding. Normally, rainwater is absorbed by the soil, but sometimes it rains so hard that the soil can't absorb all the water. During very heavy rains, huge amounts of water can rush violently down the sides of large hills or mountains. The water can also run into nearby streams or rivers and cause them to overrun their banks.

Hail is not very common, but it can occur during thunderstorms. Usually hailstones are too small and too few to cause any serious widespread problems. Sometimes, though, they come down in great numbers or they grow to an inch or more in diameter. Then they can cause damage to plants and property. Thunderstorms also can have very strong winds. Thunderstorm winds can damage trees, plants, and buildings.

The great heat from a lightning flash causes thunder. The air around the lightning is heated so much that it expands very quickly. The movement of the air creates the crashing boom we call thunder.

Thunderstorms are one of the most common types of storm. At any one moment, hundreds of them are occurring over Earth.

Hail (left) and floodwater (right) cause millions of dollars of damage every year. Hail can severely damage farm crops. Floods can destroy property and even take lives.

A tornado that forms over an ocean, lake, or other large body of water is called a waterspout. Waterspouts are usually not as strong as tornadoes, but they tend to last longer.

Tornadoes occur most often in places where very different air masses run into each other and cause strong, violent thunderstorms.

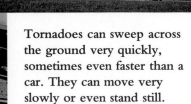

Tornadoes can sweep across the ground very quickly, sometimes even faster than a car. They can move very slowly or even stand still.

A special type of wind that happens in some thunderstorms is called a tornado. Tornadoes are tall columns of air that are spinning very fast, like a top. Tornadoes often are shaped like funnels, but sometimes they

aren't. At times, tornadoes can be over a mile wide. Other times, they can look like spinning ropes dangling out of the sides of the clouds. Tornadoes can even be invisible. When this happens, all you can see is the swirling of the bottoms of the clouds and dirt being blown around near the ground.

The winds in tornadoes are very strong. Sometimes they reach over 250 miles per hour. The winds near tornadoes can change directions so quickly that they seem to be coming from many different directions at once.

Strong winds in tornadoes can cause a lot of damage in a very short time. Pieces of straw or hay have been blown around hard enough to stick into the sides of trees. Cars and trucks have been tossed around like they were toys. Trash cans, boards, and other objects that are caught in the winds are very dangerous and can cause a lot of damage when they hit something else. Even dirt, sand and rocks can peel the paint off of cars and houses when tornadoes blow them around.

34

Tornadoes form in very strong thunderstorms. They can dip down out of the bottoms of thunderstorms with no warning. Many tornadoes form in thunderstorms that are spinning, although the storm clouds spin a lot slower than tornadoes do.

When the conditions in the atmosphere are just right for tornadoes to form, the National Weather Service issues a Tornado Watch. If there is a Tornado Watch where you are, you should keep a good lookout for any approaching thunderstorms. You might also want to stay close to a safe place where you can go if a thunderstorm or a tornado does develop.

When a tornado develops, the National Weather Service issues a Tornado Warning. This means that there is probably a tornado nearby. When a Tornado Warning is issued where you are, you should go to a safe place right away. The best place to go when this happens is somewhere low, preferably below ground.

A few places are particularly dangerous when there is a tornado nearby. Mobile homes, especially those that are not tied to the ground with special cables, are not safe in strong thunderstorms with high winds or in tornadoes. If you are in a car, you shouldn't try to outrun a tornado because it might be moving faster than you are. It is usually better to get out of the car and go to a building or other shelter.

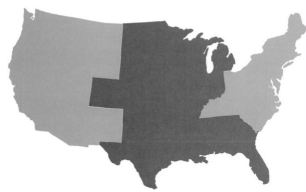

The Central and Southern United States probably have more tornadoes than any other place on Earth.

Most tornadoes occur in late afternoon or early evening during the spring and summer. They can occur almost without warning, though, anytime and anywhere.

35

Before we had satellites that could track storms, it was difficult to know where a hurricane was or where it was going. Sometimes, the only information came from ships at sea. With satellites, though, meteorologists can track a hurricane's movements very carefully.

Like most other large, violent storms, hurricanes are low pressure systems.

Hurricanes are probably the most dangerous storms. They are almost always several hundred miles across. They last for many days, travelling from one area to another.

The best way to see what a hurricane looks like is by looking at it from above. In satellite photographs, hurricanes look like huge spirals of clouds that get deeper as you go toward the center of the spiral. Right in the middle of the hurricane, you can usually see the eye, a place that has no clouds in it.

Hurricane winds get stronger as you go from the outer edges of the spiral toward the center. They can reach speeds of over 150 miles per hour. In the eye, however, the winds are very light.

A lot of things go into making a hurricane, so it is difficult to say exactly how they form. Hurricanes develop at sea close to the Equator, mainly during the late summer. When a hurricane forms, the temperature of the water is almost always over 80°F. The storm does not start strong; at first it is a lot like a group of thunderstorms. When the group of thunderstorms rotates with winds over 35 miles per hour, it is called a tropical storm. If the winds reach 75 miles per hour, the storm is officially a hurricane.

Small islands can disappear under the water when hit with a hurricane's storm surge.

In the Northern Hemisphere, the usual path a hurricane takes starts near the Equator where it forms and then moves to the west. At some point, the hurricane usually turns to the northwest, then north, and finally toward the northeast. This makes its path. look like a huge hook. It will usually move faster once it turns toward the northeast.

Hurricanes need to be over warm waters to stay strong. When a hurricane moves very far to the north where the water's temperatures are cold, it begins to weaken and eventually dies out.

Tropical storms gain energy as they take in warm, moist ocean air. This creates most of the power that drives hurricanes and makes them so dangerous.

When hurricanes reach land, they often weaken very quickly. They can still cause a lot of damage to places near the shore before they disappear. Hurricane winds can blow around tree branches, boards, and  other good-sized objects. Tornadoes sometimes occur when hurricanes first reach shore. The heavy rains in hurricanes can cause floods strong enough to wash away cars and even houses.

The biggest danger in hurricanes, though, is a storm surge. A storm surge happens when the hurricane actually lifts up part of the ocean. The pressure in a hurricane can get so low that it pulls ocean water upward. When the storm surge reaches the shore, the ocean sweeps across the land and carries buildings, cars, and anything else in its path with it.

Hurricanes leave great destruction behind them. They can even change the shape of a coastline.

STRANGE AND BEAUTIFUL SIGHTS

are an everyday part of weather. Rainbows arch across the sky after storms. The sky is a shifting backdrop of colors as the sun travels across it. It shines a pure soft blue, then a vibrant orange-red, and finally a deep thick black as the day passes. The moon rises huge and orange and slowly becomes white and small. Mirages give distant views an eerie, unreal look. White clouds roll across the skies. All around, the sky acts as an ever-changing canvas that nature paints

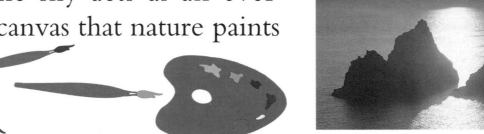

with exciting and interesting pictures. The weather offers a constant, endless source of beauty. It also offers a chance for us to learn, as we study that beauty and discover how the atmosphere creates it.

38

The sky is blue because of the way sunlight acts as it passes through the atmosphere.

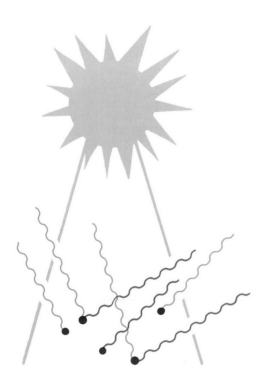

A special device called a prism can separate a beam of light into all of its colors.

The atmosphere contains trillions and trillions of molecules of all different sizes, and the sunlight is constantly running into them.

Every day, light from the sun, called *solar radiation,* strikes the top of the atmosphere and travels all the way to the ground. This radiation causes most of the atmosphere's motion and it also creates colorful rainbows, sparkling snow, and blue skies.

The sun's light reaches the top of the atmosphere in a couple of ways. Most of it travels through millions of miles of space until it reaches Earth. Solar radiation also reaches the atmosphere at night when it hits the moon and bounces back toward Earth. That's what moonlight is, and it's the reason we are able to see the moon so clearly even though it doesn't create any light of its own.

The sun's light that makes it to Earth contains many different kinds of radiation, including all the colors of light that we can see. This visible light is violet, blue, green, yellow, orange, and red all combined together.

When sunlight goes through the atmosphere, it runs into whatever happens to be in its path. The way the light reacts depends mostly on the size of the thing it strikes. If the light hits very tiny things, like the gas molecules that make up the atmosphere, then some of the colors in the sunlight scatter in all directions. If the particles that the sunlight hits are a little bit larger, more of the colors in the sunlight scatter and bounce away.

40

Light travels in waves, just like waves of water in the ocean. The waves come in different sizes, or wavelengths. Each color of light has a different wavelength. Blue and violet have a shorter wavelength than red and orange do. Because of the shorter wavelength, blue and violet light are more likely to run into molecules and bounce off of them. The wave moves up and

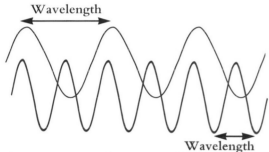

Wavelength

Wavelength

down more often over the same distance, so it is more likely to hit something. The atmosphere scatters more blue and violet light than any other type of light we can see. That is why the sky looks blue to us. We see the scattered light waves, and most of them are blue and violet.

At sunrise and sunset, the sky changes color. Parts of it actually become orange and red, the light with the longest wavelength. At these times of day, the sunlight has to go through more of the atmosphere before it gets to you than it does during the middle of the day. The light has to pass through more molecules so it is more likely that even the light with long wavelengths will run into something. More orange and red light is scattered, so the sky seems to be orange and red.

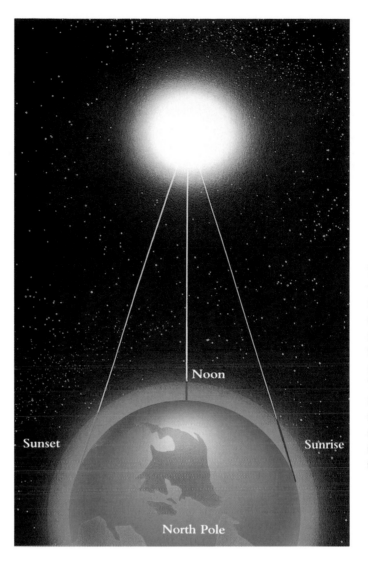

Noon

Sunset

Sunrise

North Pole

The farther a light wave travels through the atmosphere, the more likely it is that it will hit something and be reflected. The sunlight we see travels through more atmosphere at sunset and sunrise than at any other time of day.

Sunsets are usually more colorful and vibrant than sunrises. This is largely because the air contains more light-scattering particles—dust, salt, and so on—at the end of a busy day than at the end of a quiet night.

Light runs into many different things as it passes through the air, and these encounters have some beautiful results.

41

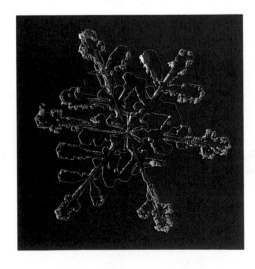

Sometimes, you may see a second rainbow outside of the first one. In the larger outer rainbow, the colors will be in the opposite order, with red on the inside and purple on the outside.

Sunlight acts quite differently when it hits a raindrop. Have you ever seen a glass of water with a straw in it? It looks like the straw bends right at the surface of the water. This illusion happens because the light bends a little when it moves out of the water and into the air.

This bending of the light is called *refraction*. The amount that the light bends depends on its color. For example, red light bends in a slightly different direction than blue light when it goes from the air into a drop of water.

If the sun is behind you and it is raining in front of you, you will see the light that is bouncing off of the backs of many of the raindrops. Since red colors leave the drops in different directions than yellow colors and green colors, you see reds in one place, greens in another place, and yellows in still another place. This is a rainbow.

Rainbows appear as arcs or even full circles. Most rainbows have red on the outside, then orange, yellow, green, and maybe blue or purple.

The bending of the light is the reason for quite a few things you might see in the atmosphere, including rainbows and mirages.

Snowflakes and clouds scatter all of the colors in sunlight. This makes them look white. If snowflakes were a lot smaller, as small as some of the molecules in the air, you wouldn't wake up on a winter morning and see white snow falling on everything. You might wake up to blue or red snow!

Light can also bend when it moves through the air. When the air is warm, sunlight moving through it bends in a different way than when the air is cold. This could make you see some very odd things, called *mirages*. When the air right near the ground is very hot, you might look at a tree in the distance and see two of them, one with the leaves at the top and another one with the leaves at the bottom. When the air right near the ground is very cold, a tree that you see in the distance might look extremely tall—much taller than it really is. These kinds of things are due to light bending in different directions as it moves through air that is different temperatures. On very hot days, you might also see what looks like a shimmering pool of water in the distance. This happens when very warm air near the ground acts like a mirror and casts a reflection of the sky.

The moon also seems to do some unusual things. It can appear to be very large when it first comes over the horizon, but it seems to shrink when it gets higher in the sky.

Meteorologists generally think that the moon looks larger near the ground because light has to go through a lot of atmosphere when it is near the horizon. This light spreads out as it goes through the air, making the moon look more spread out than it really is.

This looks like a large, shimmering pool of water. It's actually a reflection of the sky.

The atmosphere is full of wonderful sights every day. Some of them we completely understand. Other things about the world around us remain mysteries.

Some people think the moon looks bigger on the horizon because we know that it's larger than the buildings and bushes we see right next to it. Our minds are tricked into thinking it's bigger when we have things to compare it to.

GLOSSARY

Air mass: A large body of air in which conditions such as temperature, pressure, and humidity are generally the same.

Air pressure: The force created in an area by the weight of all the air above that area. Changes in air pressure are good clues about what kind of weather is coming.

Anemometer (an-uh-MAHM-uht-ur): A device that measures wind speed and direction.

Atmosphere (AT-muh-sfeer): The gases that permanently surround a planet.

Barometer (buh-RAHM-uht-ur): A device that measures the pressure of the air.

Cirrus clouds (SEER-uhs klowdz): Clouds that have a feathery, wispy appearance. Cirrus clouds are made mostly of ice crystals, and they form high in the atmosphere.

Climate (KLY-muht): A description of the average weather conditions in an area over many years.

Coalescence (ko-uh-LES-uhnts): The process of many water droplets in a cloud striking each other and joining together to form a larger droplet. If this happens enough times, a raindrop will form.

Cold front: The edge of a cold air mass that is advancing against a warm air mass. Weather conditions across a front are usually changing.

Condensation (kahn-den-SAY-shuhn): The process of water changing from a gas to a liquid. Condensation creates dew, frost, fog, and clouds.

Cumulus clouds (KYOO-myuh-luhs klowdz): Clouds that have a bulging, bumpy appearance. Cumulus clouds usually form in air that is rising quickly.

Evaporation (i-vap-uh-RAY-shuhn): The process of water changing from a liquid to a gas.

Humidity (hyoo-MID-uht-ee): The amount of water vapor in the air compared to the amount of water vapor that the air can hold.

Hurricane (HUR-uh-cayn): A large tropical storm with winds of over 74 miles an hour. Hurricanes can be hundreds of miles wide.

Meteorology (meet-ee-uh-RAHL-uh-jee): The study of Earth's atmosphere, including the study of weather and weather forecasting.

Mirage (muh-RAHZH): An illusion usually caused by light being bent or reflected as it moves from air of one temperature through air of another temperature.

Northern Hemisphere (NOR-thurn HEM-uh-sfeer): The part of Earth between the Equator and the North Pole.

Radiation (RAYD-ee-AY-shuhn): Energy released by an object in the form of waves and particles. Light is a form of radiation that we can see.

Refraction (ri-FRAK-shuhn): The bending of a wave as it moves from one medium to another, such as from air to water or from warm air to cold air. Refraction of light can create mirages and rainbows.

Riming (RYM-ing): The process of water droplets in a cloud striking a snowflake, freezing, and becoming part of the snowflake.

Southern Hemisphere (SUHTH-urn HEM-uh-sfeer): The part of Earth between the Equator and the South Pole.

Stratus clouds (STRAYT-uhs klowdz): Clouds that have a layered, sheetlike appearance. Stratus clouds usually form in air that is rising slowly.

Tornado (tor-NAYD-o): A violent, local storm of whirling winds often accompanied by a funnel-shaped cloud. Tornado winds can reach 250 miles an hour.

Warm front: The edge of a warm air mass that is advancing against a cold air mass. Weather conditions across a front are usually changing.

Wavelength (WAYV-lenkth): A measure of the distance a wave travels during a single phase or cycle.